THE SCIENCE OF A TORNADO

LINDA CERNAK

Published in the United States of America
by Cherry Lake Publishing
Ann Arbor, Michigan
www.cherrylakepublishing.com

Consultants: Jennifer Cole, Ph.D., Department of Earth and Planetary Sciences at Harvard University;
Marla Conn, ReadAbility, Inc.
Editorial direction: Red Line Editorial
Book production: Design Lab
Book design: Sleeping Bear Press

Photo Credits: Shutterstock Images, cover, 1, 7, 15, 21, 25; tornadovideo.net/AP Images, 5; Roger Nomer/The Joplin
Globe/AP Images, 8; Joe Raedle/Pool/Corbis, 9; Stefano Garau/Shutterstock Images, 11; Jim Reed/Corbis, 13; Tony
Gutierrez/AP Images, 17; NASA/NOAA GOES Project, 22; Cliff Schiappa/AP Images, 27

Library of Congress Cataloging-in-Publication Data
   CIP data has been filed and is available at catalog.loc.gov.

Cherry Lake Publishing would like to acknowledge the work of
the Partnership for 21st Century Skills. Please visit *www.p21.org*
for more information.

Printed in the United States of America
Corporate Graphics
June 2015

ABOUT THE AUTHOR

Linda Cernak has been a writer and editor of children's classroom readers and student textbooks for
more than 35 years. She has published numerous children's books about social studies, science, and
the arts. Cernak lives in Chestnut Ridge, New York, with her husband and two cats.

TABLE OF CONTENTS

WHIRLWIND IN THE MIDWEST

It was a hot and humid Sunday afternoon on May 22, 2011, in Joplin, Missouri. A local high school held its graduation ceremony. City residents shopped and worked. The weather was calm. Many were unaware that a strong, dangerous thunderstorm had entered the southwest area of the state. The thunderstorm was a violent storm called a **supercell**. It rapidly became larger and more intense. Soon, a **tornado** had formed.

At 5:11 p.m., the first sirens sounded in Joplin. They warned that a powerful storm was moving toward the

One person captured video of the tornado nearing Joplin.

city. Local television and radio stations broadcast
tornado warnings. People began to notice that the
weather was changing. The sky grew dark.

People reacted to the warnings in different ways.
Some headed for shelters. Many simply waited for more
information before deciding what to do. They did not
know how powerful the storm would be. Shortly after
5:30 p.m., the tornado touched down in Joplin. The
storm sounded like a monstrous freight train. Its
destructive path had begun.

The tornado picked up speed as it reached Joplin. Soon, the winds were spinning at more than 200 miles per hour (322 kmh). At St. John's Medical Center, staff rushed to roll patients' beds into hallways. But the tornado struck suddenly. Many people did not have time to take cover. At the hospital, the storm blew out windows and caused the electricity to fail.

The storm continued on its deadly path. It tore off a wall and most of the roof of Saint Paul's Church. It blew apart a bank so that only the vault was left

WHAT IS A SUPERCELL?

A supercell is the most violent type of thunderstorm. Supercells form when warm, moist currents of air called updrafts rise up inside storms. An updraft can reach a speed of more than 100 miles per hour (161 kmh). It can also cause clouds to rotate. From this rotation, tornadoes form.

The Joplin tornado destroyed approximately 8,000 buildings.

standing. By the time the tornado had passed, the city was in ruins. The Joplin tornado left 158 people dead. Hundreds more were injured.

The path of the tornado was 22 miles (35 km) long. Its funnel was up to 1 mile (1.6 km) wide. The tornado lasted less than half an hour. But the destruction was staggering. The storm is considered the seventh most destructive tornado in US history.

Rescue dogs helped locate tornado survivors.

After the tornado, rescue workers rushed to help survivors. Thousands of homes were leveled. Huge trees were uprooted. An estimated 300 businesses were destroyed. Cars had been tossed around like toys.

Though the destruction had ended, it would take years to rebuild the city. The tornado had demolished power lines and cell towers. People had no way of contacting family members or friends. Thousands of residents were suddenly homeless.

From the time the sirens sounded, people had about 17 minutes to take cover. This is because tornadoes can form quickly, with little warning. Their paths are unpredictable. Researchers are still studying the Joplin tornado and how it formed. They want to limit the destruction from this kind of powerful storm in the future. What they learn could help them improve tornado forecasting.

President Barack Obama met with Joplin residents after the tornado.

WHAT CAUSES A TORNADO?

A tornado is a powerful whirling column of air. It stretches from a thundercloud to the ground. Tornadoes can be up to 1 mile (1.6 km) wide.

Thunderstorms form from bright, fluffy clouds called **cumulus clouds**. Sometimes, these clouds grow wide and tall. Warm air rises from the ground and gathers in the clouds. This warm air causes the tops of the clouds to spread out. Thunderheads, or **cumulonimbus clouds**, form. Rain or hail falls, and thunder and lightning follow. Thunderstorms often

Cumulus clouds can rapidly become cumulonimbus clouds.

form along **fronts**. A front is an area where a warm air mass meets a cold air mass. Some thunderstorms that form along fronts become supercells.

As warm air rises inside a thunderhead, it produces an updraft. The updraft winds form a rotating column of air called a **mesocyclone**. The mesocyclone stretches toward the earth. The bottom of the mesocyclone becomes thinner, causing it to spin faster.

If the bottom part of a mesocyclone touches the ground, it forms a tornado. Some tornadoes also form over water. Dust and **debris** scatter as a tornado touches down on the ground. The dust and debris give the tornado its dark color. Most tornadoes have a funnel shape. Others look like twisted straws.

In 1970, **meteorologist** Tetsuya Fujita developed a scale to measure tornado strength. In 2007, scientists developed an updated version. The Enhanced Fujita (EF)

HOW A TORNADO FORMS

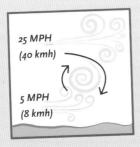

25 MPH
(40 kmh)

5 MPH
(8 kmh)

First, winds blow at different speeds. A warm air mass meets a cold air mass.

Next, the warm air forms an updraft that becomes a mesocyclone.

Last, the mesocyclone stretches toward the earth.

Scientists set up mobile equipment to gather data on how tornadoes form.

Scale ranks tornadoes from the weakest level, EF0, to the highest level, EF5. The storm in Joplin, Missouri, was an EF5 tornado. Only 5 percent of US tornadoes are above an EF3 on the scale.

As the Joplin tornado showed, tornadoes can cause severe damage in a short time. Most last for less than 10 minutes. The strength of a tornado depends on the speed of its winds. The strongest tornadoes can uproot trees. On

ENHANCED FUJITA SCALE

This scale gives a rating based on the damage a tornado causes. Most tornadoes have a rating of EF0 or EF1.

Scale	Estimated Wind Speed	Damage
EF0	Less than 73 mph (117 kmh), about as fast as a cheetah	**Light:** branches broken off trees
EF1	73–112 mph (117–180 kmh), about as fast as a fastball in professional baseball	**Moderate:** tiles broken off roofs, cars pushed around
EF2	113–157 mph (181–253 kmh), about as fast as a long-distance train	**Considerable:** entire roofs torn off houses, cars lifted off ground
EF3	158–206 mph (254–332 kmh), about as fast as a plane taking off	**Severe:** entire roofs and walls torn off homes, trains overturned
EF4	207–260 mph (333–418 kmh), about as fast as the fastest car	**Devastating:** houses destroyed, cars picked up and thrown
EF5	261–318 mph (420–512 kmh), about as fast as a high-speed train	**Incredible:** houses destroyed and swept away, heavy objects thrown in air more than 325 feet (100 m)

farms, strong tornadoes can pick up heavy animals, such as cows. **Tornadic waterspouts** have been reported to suck up entire ponds. Fish and frogs are caught up in the winds. Later, the fish and frogs "rain" down from the sky.

Changes in air temperature may weaken or end tornadoes. But scientists do not completely understand how tornadoes form and end. Researchers are continuing to study this process.

Tornadic waterspouts can be powerful, but most are weaker than land tornadoes.

CHAPTER 3

WHERE DO TORNADOES HAPPEN?

Tornadoes happen in many places around the world, including parts of Africa, Europe, Asia, and South America. However, most tornadoes occur in North America.

Tornadoes have been reported in all 50 states. They are also common in Canada. But most often, tornadoes form in the Central Plains region of the United States. This region includes an area commonly known as "Tornado Alley." It contains parts of Texas, Oklahoma, Nebraska, Iowa, Kansas, and South Dakota. Some

In 2013, an EF5 tornado hit Moore, Oklahoma, in Tornado Alley.

experts also include parts of Missouri, Illinois, Indiana, and Ohio in Tornado Alley. Many of the most violent tornadoes occur in these states.

The climate of Tornado Alley helps tornadoes to form. Weather conditions in late spring make this area prone to supercells. Warm, wet air blows in from the Gulf of Mexico. Cold, dry air moves in from the north and the Rocky Mountains. Warm, dry air moves in from the southwest. When these air masses meet, they form a front. The cool air mass slides under the warm air mass

TORNADO ALLEY CLIMATE

About one-third of all tornadoes in the United States happen in Tornado Alley. In this region, three types of air masses often meet and create thunderstorms. Sometimes, the thunderstorms cause tornadoes to form.

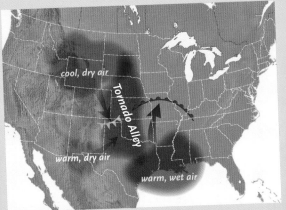

In Tornado Alley, different air masses meet and form fronts.

and pushes the warm air upward. Soon, thunderheads develop along the front. Some of those thunderheads produce supercells, which can produce tornadoes.

Sometimes, a line of thunderstorms called a squall line develops along the front. Squall lines can be more than 100 miles (161 km) long. The combination of air masses along a squall line often produces tornadoes. The air masses over Tornado Alley collide in regular patterns. No other place on Earth has these weather patterns.

IMPROVING TORNADO WARNINGS

The tornado that hit Joplin on May 22, 2011, was the first tornado since 1953 to result in more than 100 deaths. Since this tornado was especially destructive, a team of scientists studied people's responses to the tornado warnings. They hoped to find ways to improve future tornado warnings.

The team interviewed 100 Joplin survivors. Most people said that they heard the first warning siren at 5:11 p.m. This siren sounded for three minutes. Some people did not realize at first how serious the tornado was. They did not go to shelters after the first signal. Many cities in Tornado Alley use sirens to warn people about severe weather. This can include tornadoes or harmful thunderstorms. People wanted to learn more about the weather conditions before taking shelter.

The team concluded that the sirens had prevented some deaths and injuries in Joplin. But they also suggested changes to the warning system. The scientists thought that clearer alerts would encourage more people to take shelter. These alerts could give more details about the tornado, so that people could make better decisions. The scientists presented their findings to the National Weather Service. The findings will improve ways to help people respond to tornado warnings.

CHAPTER 4

TORNADO FORECASTING

Every year, tornadoes cause an average of 75 deaths in the United States. They also cause about 1,500 injuries. Weather experts want to reduce those numbers. But tornadoes today kill many fewer people than in the past. Improved warning systems give people more time to seek shelter. Tracking systems help predict when and where a tornado may happen.

In the early 1900s, weather-tracking technology was in its early stages. There was no such thing as a tornado warning. Television, weather satellites, and radar did not exist. Many people did not have radios or telephones. They could not communicate quickly if a tornado was approaching.

In the early 1950s, meteorologists began to prepare forecasts of dangerous weather. The National Weather Service opened a unit to predict storms in 1952. This unit, called the Storm Prediction Center, still exists today. Two new tools developed in the 1950s would also help predict dangerous storms. These tools were weather satellites and **Doppler radar**.

Weather stations use Doppler radar to predict storms.

On April 1, 1960, NASA launched the first weather satellite. It lifted off from Cape Canaveral in Florida. Soon after the launch, the satellite sent an image of clusters of clouds over the United States. It was the first weather satellite image. This new technology changed weather forecasting. Today, weather satellites help meteorologists

Photographs from NASA satellites help meteorologists forecast the weather.

How Science Works
Doppler Radar

Scientists use Doppler radar to predict weather. This technology uses radio waves to track storms. The waves are sent out from a weather station. They travel at a certain **frequency**. The waves strike storm clouds or precipitation. Then they bounce back to the weather station. The frequency of the waves may increase or decrease. Changes in frequency show where the storm clouds are moving. Meteorologists can tell if the clouds are moving toward or away from the station.

Doppler radar can also identify types of precipitation, including rain, hail, sleet, and snow. Scientists use it to estimate the amount of rainfall and the size of hail that people can expect. They can also forecast where the precipitation is headed.

study and track storms that might produce tornadoes. As a result, they can make more accurate forecasts.

Today, the Storm Prediction Center prepares forecasts of severe weather for all 50 states. Newer tools also help meteorologists predict storms. They can study tornadoes in laboratories. Scientists create computer models of thunderheads and mesocyclones. By studying the models, meteorologists can predict wind speed and direction. They can forecast where a tornado may touch down. Because tornadoes happen so suddenly, it is important to be able to track their movement.

Every day, meteorologists collect and study weather data. They make predictions about where strong thunderstorms will form. If a front develops in an area

TORNADOES IN CITIES

Most tornadoes in the United States have affected small towns and rural areas. However, experts say that tornadoes can also strike big cities. Since many people live close together in cities, the damage would be catastrophic. Researchers say that if an EF5 tornado hit Chicago, it could cost $20 billion in damages.

A powerful supercell develops in Tornado Alley.

with the possibility of supercells, they announce a
tornado watch. This announcement warns people of
weather conditions that might produce a tornado.
Meteorologists announce a tornado warning when a
tornado has been detected. At that point, sirens in the
area may sound. When people hear about a tornado
warning in their area, they should seek shelter.

CHAPTER 5

TORNADO SAFETY

New technologies have increased tornado warning times. In the 1980s, people had an average warning time of 5 minutes before a tornado hit. Today, the average warning time is 13 minutes.

Tornado safety plans can save lives. The most important precaution is to decide where to take shelter. A basement is the safest place to stay. If a home does not have a basement, people should hide under a stairway or in a closet.

Sometimes, people are outside when a tornado hits. Experts say they should head for the nearest shelter. A

A community tornado shelter in Wichita, Kansas, protects people from flying debris.

second option is to look for a low place to hide. People should leave their cars. Tornadoes can send vehicles sailing through the air.

Some homeowners construct small "safe rooms" to protect people from debris. Others build underground shelters with steel doors. Many modern homes can withstand winds of up to 110 miles per hour (177 kmh). Better building construction has decreased tornado damage. Cities and states often have building codes to protect homes from storms.

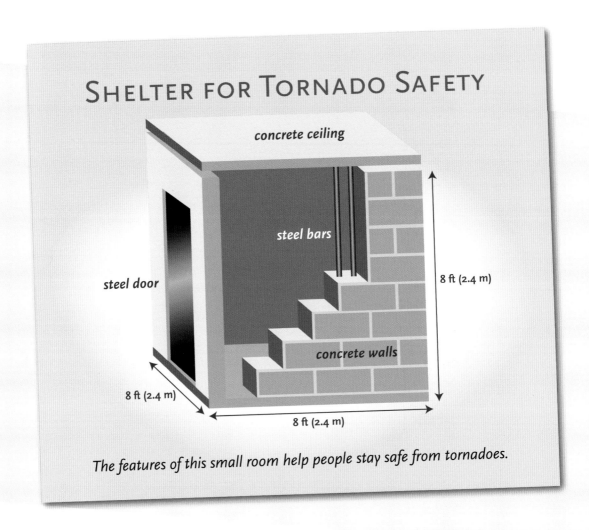

SHELTER FOR TORNADO SAFETY

concrete ceiling

steel bars

steel door

8 ft (2.4 m)

concrete walls

8 ft (2.4 m)

8 ft (2.4 m)

The features of this small room help people stay safe from tornadoes.

Weather technology has improved people's ability to prepare for tornadoes. However, there is still a lot about tornadoes that scientists do not understand. More research will help scientists improve tornado warning times.

Warn on Forecast

The National Oceanic and Atmospheric Administration (NOAA) is a government agency that studies weather. NOAA has established a program called Warn on Forecast to increase severe weather warning times. However, scientists need to learn more about the weather conditions that produce a tornado.

To find the information, NOAA began a research project called VORTEX2. More than 100 scientists, students, and workers go to an area where a supercell storm might happen. Then they use instruments to collect data about wind speed and direction. They even gather data inside storms. From this information, scientists hope to understand more about how tornadoes form.

Top Five Worst
US Tornadoes

1. **March 18, 1925: The Tristate Tornado**
   The deadliest tornado in US history traveled across the states of Missouri, Illinois, and Indiana. The Tristate Tornado caused 695 deaths and more than 2,000 injuries.

2. **May 6, 1840: The Great Natchez Tornado**
   This tornado hit Natchez, Mississippi, resulting in 317 deaths and 109 injuries. At least 60 flat boats were lifted into the air and later sunk in the Mississippi River.

3. **May 27, 1896: The Great St. Louis Tornado**
   Within 20 minutes of striking St. Louis, this tornado caused about 1,000 injuries. There were about 255 deaths. The tornado traveled for 10 miles (16 km), leaving a path of more than 300 destroyed buildings.

4. **April 5, 1936: Tupelo, Mississippi**
   In early April 1936, tornadoes hit homes in several southern states. The deadliest was an EF5 tornado in Tupelo that caused a total of 216 deaths and more than 700 injuries.

5. **April 6, 1936: Gainesville, Georgia**
   The day after the Tupelo tornado, three tornadoes hit Gainesville, Georgia. Some of the worst destruction occurred at the Cooper Pants factory. Shortly after the tornado hit, the building collapsed. Seventy workers died.

LEARN MORE

FURTHER READING

Carson, Mary Kay. *Inside Tornadoes*. New York: Sterling, 2010.

Fradin, Judith Bloom, and Dennis Brindell Fradin. *Tornado! The Story Behind These Twisting, Turning, Spinning, and Spiraling Storms*. Washington, DC: National Geographic Children's Books, 2012.

Miller, Ron. *Chasing the Storm: Tornadoes, Meteorology, and Weather Watching*. Minneapolis: Twenty-First Century Books, 2014.

WEB SITES

National Geographic: Tornadoes
http://environment.nationalgeographic.com/environment/natural-disasters/tornado-profile
This Web site includes tornado safety tips and videos of actual tornadoes.

Severe Weather 101: Tornadoes
http://www.nssl.noaa.gov/education/svrwx101/tornadoes
This Web site features facts about tornadoes, including how they are detected and forecasted.

GLOSSARY

cumulonimbus clouds (kyoo-myuh-loh-NIM-buhs KLOWDS) large, dark clouds that can produce thunderstorms and severe weather

cumulus clouds (KYOO-myuh-luhs KLOWDS) bright, puffy clouds that can form thunderheads

debris (DUH-bree) ruins or pieces of broken things

Doppler radar (DOP-ler RAY-dahr) a radar system used to predict weather

frequency (FREE-kwuhn-see) the number of waves that pass a certain point in a second

fronts (FRUHNTS) areas where warm and cold air masses meet

mesocyclone (mez-oh-SAHY-klohn) a swirling column of air inside a thunderhead

meteorologist (MEE-tee-or-ah-low-jist) a person who predicts and reports on the weather

supercell (SOO-per-sel) a large and violent thunderstorm

tornadic waterspouts (tor-NAH-dik WAH-tur-spowts) tornadoes that form over water

tornado (tor-NAY-doh) a powerful rotating column of air that extends from a thunderstorm to the ground

tornado warnings (tor-NAY-doh WORN-ingz) weather alerts announced when tornadoes are detected

tornado watch (tor-NAY-doh WOCH) a weather alert announced when a storm might produce tornadoes

INDEX